it's a dog's life

it's a dog's life

humorous and meaningful quotes on life

edited by andrew yelland

Published in the United States in 2005
by Tangent Publications
an imprint of
Axis Publishing Limited
8c Accommodation Road
London NW11 8ED
www.axispublishing.co.uk

Creative Director: Siân Keogh
Editorial Director: Anne Yelland
Production Manager: Jo Ryan

ISBN: 1–904707–26–2

2 4 6 8 10 9 7 5 3 1

Printed and bound in China

about this book

It's a Dog's Life brings together an inspirational selection of powerful, life-affirming, and humorous phrases about dogs, and their characteristics and antics, and combines them with evocative and gently amusing photographs.

We all lead busy lives and sometimes forget to pause and appreciate how amusing, and inspirational dogs can be. These examples of wit and wisdom, written by real people and based on their true-life experiences of their pets, sum up the pleasure of owning a dog and watching as it goes about its daily life.

A quick glance at this book will confirm why it is no wonder that dogs are still "man's (and woman's) best friend" to so many people.

about the author

Andrew Yelland has worked in publishing for several years, and specializes in titles on pets and pet care, in addition to such popular subjects as cinema, theater, and gardening. From the many hundreds of thoughts and sayings that were sent to him by pet lovers from around the world, he has selected those that best sum up what a dog's life is all about—its ups and downs, trials and tribulations, and the qualities and traits that make dogs so special to their owners.

Red meat isn't bad
for you: blue-green
meat is another
matter.

Desserts is stressed spelled backward.

A positive mental attitude will annoy enough people to make it worth the effort.

Do radioactive cats
have 18 half-lives?

It's always darkest just before dawn so that is the best time to steal your next-door neighbor's newspaper.

The problem with being punctual is that there's never anyone around to appreciate it.

A sense of humor is
common sense dancing.

Cheese is merely milk's shot at immortality.

I get enough exercise just
pushing my luck.

I went shopping for camouflage trousers last week, but couldn't find any.

Whoever said
"let sleeping dogs lie"
didn't sleep with dogs.

The reason a dog has so many friends is that he wags his tail instead of his tongue.

Did you ever stop
to think, and forget
to start again?

I didn't say it
was your fault.
I said I was going
to blame you.

Vegetables are a must on a diet—carrot cake, pumpkin pie, and mushroom pizza.

When you don't know what you
are doing, do it neatly.

We are born naked, wet, and hungry—and then it gets worse.

You are unique, just like everybody else.

No human could ever love
you as much as I do.

Never ask a barber if he thinks you need a haircut.

I must hurry, for there go my people and I am their leader.

To err is human,
to forgive canine.

If you think you have any influence, try ordering someone else's dog around.

A face can say many things—
especially the mouth part.

Where there's a will,
I want to be in it.

Every dog may have his day—but it's the puppies that have the weekends.

Dogs think humans are nuts.

If you want the best chair
in the house, you will have
to move the dog first.

When everything is coming at you, you are in the wrong lane.

We have enough youth,
could we please now have
a fountain of smart?

Genius does what it must,
talent does what it can,
and you had best do
what I tell you.

Running makes
the ground feel
needed.

Take my advice—I don't use it anyway.

A dog is a miracle
with paws.

The severity of an itch is inversely proportional to my ability to reach it.

Who tested my new improved flavor dog food?

Always leave room in your schedule for a good nap.

A procrastinator's work
is never done.

Nothing is foolproof to a sufficiently talented fool.

The first rule of
tinkering is to save
all the parts.

He who smiles in a crisis
has found someone
else to blame.

I am a nobody, nobody is perfect, therefore I am perfect.

My opinions may have changed,
but not the fact that I am right.

If the boss has no daughters, you'll need ability to get to the top.

Without geography,
you are nowhere.

The fatter the flea
the leaner the dog.

Love your enemies…

…it is sure to make them mad.

If you stare at someone long enough, eventually you'll get what you want.

If anything is attractive, useful, and expensive, they stopped making it yesterday.

To find the
skateboard, walk
around the house
in the dark.

There are three types
of people, those who
can count and those
who can't.

A stick is simply a boomerang
that doesn't work.

A man who has everything
needs a woman to show
him how to work it.

Multitasking is doing several
things badly at once.

I am your best friend now
and forever…

…especially
when you have food.

Reach for the stars, even if you have to stand on a cactus.

All generalizations are bad.

It's lonely at the top,
but you eat better.

Attitude—a little thing that
makes a big difference.

A barking dog never bites.